A Short Guide to Hospitable Writing

by

Eugenie Rounds Rayner, MA

Branch Hill Publications

Bennington, Vermont

A Short Guide to Hospitable Writing is an expanded compilation of some previously published writings of Eugenie Rounds Rayner that appeared in various venues. This is a companion to The Magic Lamp website at http://www.magiclampedits.wordpress.com

Published by Branch Hill Publications,

Bennington, Vermont.

ISBN-13: 978-0692526163

ISBN-10: 0692526161

A-ZBook Reviews columns creative process Creativity critique drafts editing Exercise genres grammar petpeevestravel Welcome writing

Also by the author

Song of the Blessing Trees
God's I AM in You (co-author, expanded and edited)*

Books edited include:

Hope's Shadow
Evolution of a Conceptual God: Navigating the Landmines
Wind in the Wine*
Crystal Promise: The Shattered Crystal, Book 1*
Vicious Bites (also contributor and Afterword)
Feltboard Revival*
Dry Branch Hollow and Other Stories*
Song of the Earth*
Stand on Your Own Two Feet*
A Wee Little Man
Fatizen 24602*
To Give a Rose*
Liturgical Ministries Customary, Episcopal Diocese of
Vermont (also contributor)
On the Wings of Seasons (Fall 2015)

Titles marked with asterisks are published by Branch Hill
Publications. See the Website and book catalogue at
www.branchhillpublications.weebly.com for more details.

The pages are still blank, but there is a miraculous feeling of the words being there, written in invisible ink and clamoring to become visible.

Vladimir Nabokov

Thank You

The online writing groups known as Vicious Writers and then Key Publications were the genesis of my official professional editing work, so many thanks to founder Damian Gray for sending folks my way and for spreading the word through his generous recommendations.

Thanks to Jim Vires for his formatting skills and expertise for Branch Hill Publishing, both for this book and all the books we've published. And special thanks to Jim for his suggestion of one little word change that made such a difference.

And, of course, thank you to all who support and encourage Magic Lamp Edits and me in so many ways!

***

You are never too old to set another goal or to dream a new dream.

C. S. Lewis

I admire anybody who has the guts to write anything at all.

E. B. White

This book is dedicated to all who write, who dream of writing, anything at all. I appreciate and applaud you who want to explore the world around us and the worlds within, and your courage and passion as you craft word after word for all the rest of us. Thank you!

Table of Contents

Introduction

If you look up 'hospitality of writing' or 'hospitality in writing' or 'hospitable writing' on Google.com, the most that comes up is things like B & Bs for writing retreats or conferences. To date I have found nothing that corresponds to what I mean by hospitable writing, and that is why I decided to put together this little guide.

William Zinsser's classic adage encapsulates the concept in a nutshell: 'Hard writing makes for easy reading. Easy writing makes for hard reading.' As a writer *and* an editor, I believe that part of a writer's task is to make one's reading audience as comfortable as possible, even if the subject matter isn't all that comforting.

An editor's job is essentially the same, only more so. A good editor should wear at least three hats: 1) work with and on behalf of the author to keep his/her voice authentic and true to his/her intent; 2) work on behalf of the readers – for instance, has the author used the best points-of-view for the characters, are the technical parts correct (spelling, grammar, punctuation, tenses, and so on), or does anything need to be rearranged? and 3)work on behalf of the relationship that develops between writers and the reading community.

Just like a host has to prepare his or her house before s/he welcomes guests, editors prepare others' writing to attract and receive readers. While a host metaphorically rolls out a red carpet of comfort and ease, we editors make of our trade a magic carpet for the same purpose.

In my case, I try to provide a magic lamp as well (a play on the story of Aladdin's lamp because of the spelling of my nickname, Genie). My primary wish is to provide a comfortable reading atmosphere, both in my own writing and that of others. That hospitality is important to me because relationship is its driving force.

I've long believed that writing is – at least in part – about relationship and connecting with others. Otherwise, why do we write? We may argue with something someone has written, or we may love it, but either way we've established a two-way relationship. I don't know about you, but I'd much rather have an argument with one or more readers – and that has happened – than have no response because of disinterest.

This little book, then, is a compilation of columns and blog posts from, and companion to, my Website, most of which have been expanded for this publication, along with some new material. Blog posts here have the blue titles. The other chapters here are on my site as 'pages.' Most of these were columns originally written for ezines or groups that were part of two related online writing groups to which I belonged, and for which I served as senior director of hospi … er, editor.

So, if I may be allowed to mix my metaphors, welcome to my 'house.' Thank you for your visit, and please make yourself comfortable. And to whet your appetite, a few *bon mots* …

*****

A comfort zone is a beautiful place, but nothing ever grows there. (Unattributed meme on Facebook)

Start writing, no matter what. The water does not flow until the faucet is turned on. (Louis L'Amour)

I hate writing, I love having written. (Dorothy Parker)

Don't forget – no one else sees the world the way you do, so no one else can tell the stories that you have to tell. (Charles de Lint)

A non-writing writer is a monster courting insanity. (Franz Kafka)

A writer is someone who has taught his mind to misbehave. (Oscar Wilde)

Fill your paper with the breathings of your heart. (William Wordsworth)

A story should have a beginning, a middle and an end, but not necessarily in that order. (Jean-Luc Godard)

If I fall asleep with a pen in my hand, don't remove it – I may be writing in my dreams. (Terri Guillemets, The Writer's Circle)

*****

Handy Work

This is an exercise that I've used to start new writing groups and gatherings. It's an easy way to introduce folks to each other (when necessary), but its primary intent is to induce the giggle factor and get our whole brain working. Some participants have told me it's the one time they can slow down enough to catch all the words that swirl around in their brains.

So sit where you're comfortable and prepare a writing space. *Take 10-15 minutes and write something – anything – **with your non-dominant hand**.*

Simple! The beauty of this little workout is many-fold. It exercises the side of our brain that we don't normally use much or intentionally and thus flexes different creative muscles. No one else has to see our handwriting in this exercise. It gets us away from the computer for a little bit. It can be used with pen/pencil and paper or paintbrush and canvas. Doodling and drawing circles work just as well if we can't think of anything to write, or we can copy something.

You can do this as often as you want during the day, even with actions that don't involve writing. Try eating with your non-dominant hand. Or pour something into a glass. Can anyone brush your teeth with your other hand?!? *{Disclaimer: I cannot be held responsible for spilled milk or messy toothpaste – or any other – accidents should you choose to try these suggestions.}*

As a start, try writing to-do lists or grocery lists with your non-dominant hand. The more things we try, the better and more comfortable we get with such endeavors. That will and does benefit our writing. An added bonus — I've found that sometimes this little exercise helps when I hit the proverbial 'wall,' because it stimulates all kinds of creative ideas.

Have fun with your handy work!

Hospitable Writing: A Book Review of Sorts

Last night I finished reading a book that really needed an editor. Or, rather, a better editor.

This non-fiction book was wildly popular when it was first published by a major publisher in the early 1990s, and it is still well-known among women of a certain age. I bought the book years ago when I intended to use it as a reference in a course of study. That study never happened, so the book sat on my shelves and made several moves with me. Along the way, I started to read it a couple of times, but I just couldn't get into it and put it aside after a short while, never getting past the first chapter.

When I picked it up again a few months ago, I had to *make* myself get deeper into the book, which is almost 500 pages long. The subject matter still matters to me and I'm glad I made the effort to stay with it. I'll even pass the book on to a friend or two, but I will do so with a caveat because both of these women are well-read and one is a writer: try not to get bogged down in the book's inhospitable writing and presentation.

What makes a book hospitable? In my view, perhaps stemming from my southern upbringing, a book should be inviting. A writer should welcome readers and strive to make them comfortable, even if the subject matter is a difficult one. For example, this book could be shorter in length. Maybe not by much, but even 100 fewer pages would help. Long books are usually no problem for me —

some of my favorites, both fiction and non-fiction, are far longer — but this author repeats herself quite often, and most of the time it is unnecessary.

The author's usually dense, sometimes complicated, sentence structure meant I had to read too many sentences more than twice (yes, twice) to glean her meaning. Some of this is due to her multi-lingual heritage — Spanish and Eastern European, in addition to English — but most of the time this could have been alleviated by a simple comma or two, or making a long sentence into two. I wonder, in fact, if the narrative was transcribed from tapes[1] because of the sometimes-fast and breathless style. Still, I believe a better editor could have kept her rich language structures intact, even vibrant, while making the book more comfortable for a reading audience.

To the author's credit, the book is well-researched and her notes and references are extensive. She is a well-known Jungian scholar and practitioner with a PhD, and her *bona fides* show throughout. The subject matter is one I've long been interested in, which is why I kept the book and why I kept reading through to the end, even when I had to struggle on occasion. For such a long book, the typography and formatting are surprisingly well done, although the fonts are necessarily smaller and line spacing tighter than I find most comfortable.

In addition to the above considerations, then, what else helps make a book hospitable? Readers will differ, of course, but it helps to think about what works and what doesn't. Something as simple as plenty of white space is important for me (see the last sentence in the previous

---

[1] This particular book was the author's first published printed work. Her previous body of work was on audiotapes.

paragraph) and is just one more example. The more white space, the more the eye can 'rest' and make easier transitions from paragraph to paragraph, chapter to chapter.

Ultimately it comes down to William Zinsser's declaration: 'Hard writing makes for easy reading. Easy writing makes for hard reading.' I submit that one can — and should — switch 'editing' for 'writing,' too.

When *both* missions, hard writing and easy reading, are achieved, it's a good bet the book — or story, essay, academic paper or dissertation, even a blog post — is one you can be comfortable with and you can rest in its hospitality as you read.

Apostrophe Alert

Once upon a time, a friend of mine used to carry in her capacious, overflowing purse a dark permanent marker that had one purpose and one purpose only. No matter where they appeared or on what, this was her mission: to eradicate any and all erroneously-placed apostrophes with which she came into contact. Sometimes she had trouble finding pens or datebook or the like, but she always knew where that marker was and she never hesitated to use it.

True story. She was so dedicated to her cause that she was almost an apostrophe vigilante, and woe betide the person(s) who argued with her right to correct any miscreant little squiggles. No one could ever win, though, because she knew her apostrophes and she knew she did.

Those innocent little vertical punctuation marks drive everyone crazy, but the difference a correctly-placed apostrophe makes can be important. So let's go a few rounds with my friend and see if she'd need her permanent marker for our own writing.

The 1960's was a decadent decade.
The 1960s was a decadent decade.

Turn left at the Knapps' house.
Turn left at the Knapp's house.

Please bring in the plants tonight!
Please bring in the plant's tonight!

There are more examples below, but this is a good start. I have no doubt all readers and writers are quick to note that the second example, the third line, and the fifth line are the correct ways to use – or *not* use – apostrophes in these specific instances.

If one uses an apostrophe in a date, as well as the final line of the examples, the apostrophe denotes ownership. So you might ask yourself as you write, 'the 1960's ... what? What did they own?' The same thing with the plant example: if we write 'bring in the plant's ...' an editor will (or should) say 'bring in the plant's what? The plant's dirt? Bugs?' In this case too, the apostrophe indicates a single plant; the correct example on the left obviously shows there are more plants than one.

One of the examples in the middle is much too prevalent in today's writing world. Again we've got an issue of ownership, which in this case is correct to connote; at the same time there's the singular/plural agreement and punctuation to deal with. What to do, what to do?

Easy answer: if there is more than one person, the apostrophe almost always goes *after* the 's'. Otherwise you'd turn left at 'that (singular) old Knapp's house.' He or she may be singular in many ways, but a punctuation problem shouldn't be one of them. If there are two or more Knapps and we need to indicate ownership, then the apostrophe goes after the 's' and should never separate them. Of course you can take the easy way out and write "Turn left at the Knapp residence."

(Notice there is no apostrophe in my latter use of *Knapps*. The same holds true if I write of my own family with no need to indicate ownership: *The Rayners are the nicest people in the world. They're almost as nice as the Smiths.*

Whether you agree with that assertion or not, none of those three family groups needs an apostrophe when mentioned as a whole.)

Here are some real-life examples (I made up those other ones based on usages I've seen), so get out your own editor's red pen or blue pencil – or maybe even a permanent marker – and give my friend a run for her money. Some of the following are correct, some are not. See how you do and then check your answers with those at the bottom.

From *Yahoo!* news headlines:

1) *Italian police seize mafia boss' pet crocodile.*

2) *White House threat to kids' summer vacation.*

A newspaper classified ad:

3) *Looking for kids motorcycle gear.*

Newspaper headlines:

4) *Body of heiress' likely found in river.*

5) *Farmers' market seeks new manager.*

6) *Vermont earns straight [financial] A's.*

From a newspaper story:

7) *... [A] friend of Ellis' family ... was blunter in his observations.*

Since that was so much fun – well, it is for editors and apostrophe vigilantes :-)! – try this one.

Its too hard to keep up with you're neighbors, the Jones'.

The three apostrophe mistakes in that sentence (which I made up) should be readily apparent. Change that sentence to read *It's too hard to keep up with your neighbors, the Joneses,* and you'll have happier readers and a happier editor.

Why the differences?

It's is a contraction for 'it is.' If we write 'its' with no apostrophe, there is no meaning in this particular sentence. 'Its' with no apostrophe fits with such things as "the car lost its brakes" or "the plant stand looks better in its original color." I know – technically these are ownership concepts, but inanimate objects don't (usually) own anything, so there is no apostrophe. When in doubt, always write the sentence both ways: with and without a contraction and use the one that makes sense.

In the correct sentence, *your* is not a contraction so there is no apostrophe. If you put the apostrophe in – which is a common mistake with this one – the word will mean 'you are.' It doesn't make much sense in the sentence then. Do the contraction trick here, too: Does it make sense to say 'It's too hard to keep up with you are neighbors the Joneses'?

And the Joneses? Because their name already ends in an 's,' the apostrophe is superfluous and not needed.[2] If we

---

[2] There is disagreement about this among grammarians and editors. Some agree with me, others don't. I stand by my assertion, however.

have to give directions to their house instead of the Knapps' house, we write "Turn left at the Joneses' house."

Now that you're thoroughly confused, I want to note that my word processing program is, too. Which brings up a good point: don't always trust those red, blue, and green alert lines! They do bring things to your attention, but they're not always right. When I wrote *Knapps' house* above, the invisible grammar police inside my program indicate that's wrong. Trust me instead: it's *not* wrong.

They're tiny and they're tricky, but those little apostrophes pack a big punch. We can't hear or see them when we speak; the differences they make in our writing, though, are important. We owe it to our readers to get those little devils right. And just think: if your writing is destined for submission and uses apostrophes correctly, your work will rise faster to the top of that pile on your potential editor's desk (or editors' desks)!

Answers:

1) This should read *Italian police seize mafia boss's pet crocodile.*

2) This is correct.

3) That person should look for *kids' motorcycle gear* or rewrite it to read *Looking for motorcycle gear for kids.*

4) No apostrophe is necessary as this is written. If the copy editor is determined to include an apostrophe, then the headline should read *Heiress's body likely found in river.*

5) This is correct for the same reason #2 is right: plural farmers' apostrophes work the same as plural kids' do.

6) Vermont's financial grade is better than the paper's editing grade: there should be no apostrophe after the *A*.

7) Like the mafia boss and the heiress, this should have an 's' after the apostrophe so it reads *A friend of Ellis's family* ...

Bring it On!

Or should that be 'take it on'?

My father was an old-style grammar purist, and his all-time pet peeve was when people said or wrote 'bring' when they meant 'take.' An example: I'm on the phone with my sister today and say, 'I'll bring potato salad to the cookout tomorrow.'

Technically, one can argue that I'll bring it with me when I come to the cookout, but because I'm not now en route — and I'm planning *to go* — it should be 'I'll take potato salad … tomorrow.' The cookout has yet to happen, so I'm planning to take the potato salad. If I'm on the phone with her right this minute and headed out the door, *then* I can say 'I'm bringing the potato salad' since the 'with me as I come' is understood.

When my sister and I were growing up, this became something of a family joke with our dad. Usually we were careful to use the right word if Dad was within earshot, but as we got older, we'd sometimes do the opposite to get a rise out of him. It didn't take him long to catch on, of course, and my mother, sister and I all had fun baiting him just to see his eyes twinkle.

I confess that I've taken a less purist tack for some years now, even before Dad died, but only in spoken conversation. If I'm writing and/or editing, I pay much more attention and I'm careful to use the correct word in the appropriate context.

Would that I could take that to the bank, but at least I know it would bring a twinkle to my dad's eyes.

Me, Myself, and I

Between you and me, the pronouns in the title above give this editor a major headache for one simple reason: they are misused much too often.

Because colloquial speech has set the pattern – especially on televised news shows, where the journalists should, in my opinion, know better – it's more and more common to find incorrect pronouns in writers' works as well. It's probably not a good idea to correct someone when they're talking, but I hope this column will help writers reduce their editors' need for the aspirin tablets.

Here's a sampler of popular pronoun usage, all gleaned from actual conversations:

- Her and I are going to the beach today.
- They can't rely on Genie and I to do all that!
- Joe and myself have too much to do today to wash the car.
- Him and I have enough material to put on our own show.
- Me and her need to meet for lunch tomorrow.
- Sheila and me used to write together all the time.
- You and me won the contest!

You get the idea, and they probably sound familiar. Here's the thing: not one of those is correct! Let's try these instead:

- *She and I* are going to the beach today.
- They can't rely on *Genie and me* to do all that!

- *Joe and I* have too much to do today to wash the car.
- *He and I* have enough material to put on our own show.
- *She and I* need to meet for lunch tomorrow.
- *Sheila and I* used to write together all the time.
- *You and I* won the contest!

One thing to remember is this: each of the first set of examples mixes up first, second or third person personal pronouns in the same sentence, and that's a no-no.

Leonard Rosen, grammar maven and author of *The Everyday English Handbook* (pg. 81)[3], explains it much better than I (can). "A subjective case pronoun can be used as the subject of a sentence. When using pronouns in a compound sentence, be sure that the pronouns are expressed in the subjective case:

"You should be more careful.

"Freddy and *she* stopped by for a visit.

"A subjective case pronoun can be the subject complement of a sentence, following the linking verb *to be* (expressed in the forms *is, are, was,* and *were*).

"Barbara can paint more efficiently than *he* (can paint).

"Benny remembered Eric better than *I* (remembered Eric).

"Benny remembered Eric better than (he remembered) *me.*"

---

[3] This is a good resource to keep on your writing desk.

"(Note the difference in meaning between the last two sentences. In the final sentence, an objective case pronoun, 'me,' is used, since it is the object of the unstated verb, 'remembered.')

"When a pronoun is part of an appositive phrase that renames the subject of a sentence, use the subjective case:

"The committee — Jeanette, Linda and *I* — took the afternoon off and went to lunch.

"(The appositive renames the subject 'committee.' Therefore, a subjective case pronoun, 'I,' must be used in the appositive.)

"BUT

"When a pronoun functions as a subject in the second part of a comparison, use the subjective case. (The words in parentheses are implied by the comparison.)

"Steven is as fearless as *she* (is fearless).

"(The pronouns *she* and *I* take the place of proper nouns, such as Susan or Adrienne, which rename the subjects of the sentences, 'this' and 'it.')

"This is *she*.

"It is *I*.

"*He* is a good friend.

"*We* went to the concert."

Got all that? I don't know about you, but my head is swimming with all these grammatical terms! To be honest, I can't remember what an appositive phrase is without looking it up, but I know when it's right or wrong. I do know it can be hard to differentiate between and among these and other finer points of grammar, but it is worth it in the long run.

I think the confusion comes when we think "I'm meeting her at the beach" or for lunch. But if we take just a moment to rework the sense of the sentence, what we want to convey, who all is involved, and to remember our basic lessons from 7th grade grammar class, then it gets easier. Sort of.

It's all a matter of agreement. Think of how you would write – or say – these or similar sentences if another person weren't involved. Would you say, for instance, "Myself has too much to do today"? or "Her is going to the beach"? or "Me is meeting someone for lunch"? Not hardly!

So pay attention to your pronouns, those of you and your friends. When all else fails, ask yourself where and how 'you' and 'they' fit in your sentences, spoken or written. Your readers – and your editors – will thank you for taking the time to do so.

Novelties

Writing a novel is like driving a car at night. You can only see as far as your headlights, but you can make the whole trip that way.

E. L. Doctorow

This new novel gets harder to write the farther along I go. I'm on Chapter 16 now, and it's taken me a couple of weeks just to get to the third page.

The first several chapters of this first draft went faster than I expected, at least compared to my first novel if you know that it took almost 20 years to write that one (which is almost a story in itself). Along about Chapter 12, though, things started to slow way down, and now I'm lucky if I can eke out a couple of paragraphs or a few lines of dialogue a day. Doctorow's headlights aren't reaching very far lately.

As frustrating as that is, especially when all writing conditions are good — everything's quiet, the dogs are cooperating, the phone's not ringing — I've learned not to get impatient. When I was a licensed lay preacher in the Episcopal Church, I found that some of my best sermons were those that were squeezed out one or two sentences at a time, with substantial breaks in between.

So I've gone back to what helped then: I get up and walk around, put the dishes and/or laundry away, start a new load in the washing machine, fix some tea, go outside and listen to the cardinal(s) sing, scratch behind the dog's big floppy ears, make the bed, make something to eat or get something to munch on, smoke a cigarette (I know …), take a short walk when the weather allows, check email, post a new blog entry (ahem) … You get the idea.

It's not procrastination. It really isn't. It's procrastination if I do one or more of all those things *before* I sit down to write. If you're a writer and you're reading this, you know what I mean. Those little breaks give our brains — and our bodies — a breather and, if we're lucky, another line or two of dialogue pops into our heads. Or the arc that we need to get over that hump in the storyline appears fully written out behind our eyes. We can almost feel the literal or figurative fresh air unclog the jumble. What a difference! Now we can work with the grace of a new perspective.

So we run back to the computer, type those beautiful words in, and … wait. Again. And light up another cigarette. Or make another cup of tea or coffee.

… Oh, I just realized it's almost lunchtime. And my goodness, that is one happy cardinal out there ...

The words will come when I need them. It's not every day that the cardinal's melody is so close by. I know my characters will pardon me while I just sit and listen to his beautiful song.

The Shades of Semicolons

Here is a lesson in creative writing. First rule: Do not use semicolons. They are transvestite hermaphrodites representing absolutely nothing. All they do is show you've been to college.

Kurt Vonnegut

That quote from Vonnegut sparked a lively discussion among a group of writers on Facebook recently. What follows is some of the conversation.

Response: "Sorry, Vonnegut, but semicolons actually represent a shade of silence. Hating semicolons is idiotic. Why shouldn't we use the entire spectrum of pauses and silences available to us?"

Genie: " _____ is right! There's a definite place for semicolons; the trick is finding the right one."

Response: "Well, these absolutes don't hold water. Stephen King says, 'Adverbs are your enemy,' but they have their place when consumed in moderation."

Response: "Second rule … Kurt Vonnegut can do whatever he wants; I can do whatever I want, too."

Response: "Use short sentences, never use semicolons and whatever you do never depend on your own editing or computer editing."

Genie: "I agree with the first and third statements, especially the one about computer editing. And I'll add 'use short, simple words' to that. If we change the second to 'use semicolons judiciously,' then I can agree with that one too. [The image] of a 'shade of silence' is perfect, and no other punctuation captures it in the same way. But they should be used sparingly and never, ever in place of a comma or colon. IMHO, of course ..."

In my far from humble opinion, the semicolon is a much maligned and much misused little punctuation mark. It doesn't serve the same purpose as a comma; nor does it take the place of a colon, and therein lies the rub. Commas indicate a brief pause to separate clauses, thoughts and parts of written conversation ("You're so beautiful," he said). Colons are intended to get the readers' attention, as a heads-up that something important is on its way. Semicolons, on the other hand, have their own beauty and simplicity.

Think of it like breathing. Commas are the quick, shallow breaths that move our writing – and reading – along; colons are the deep breaths that slow us down and bring fresh air to our work to stimulate the construction of our words and thoughts; and semicolons are somewhere in between.

That 'shades of silence' metaphor *is* perfect, because there are times when neither the comma nor the colon provides the right amount of oxygen to our words. It doesn't – and shouldn't – happen very often, but there are times when a sentence needs to take a deeper breath than a comma but not as deep as a colon, and that's when the semicolon is needed.

Leonard Rosen explains that "The semicolon signals a pause longer than a comma but briefer than a period." In *The Everyday English Handbook,* Rosen explains the various ways semicolons are used: between independent clauses in a long compound sentence; for emphasis; in a series of items that contain punctuation "and/or when they are especially long" [as I've done here]; to coordinate conjunctions and adverbial "conjunctions that normally join two independent clauses"; and more (pgs 128- 130).

It's important to note that semicolons should NOT be used when writing conversations or narrative in our fictional works. As one of my wise mentors told me, we can't 'see' semicolons in our verbal speech with one another. The same holds true in our characters' dialogues. Semicolons should be – IMHO – reserved for non-fiction writing.

What about using semicolons in poetry? Well, that's a whole 'nother kettle of fish altogether. Frankly, I never use them in my poems. I use dashes or ellipses instead because some of my poetry is designed to be read aloud and performed, so I use punctuation that serves as stage directions for me. If I post or submit that same poetry, I change the punctuation for easier reading by others. Poetry is so personal and subjective, each person must decide what kind of punctuation makes his or her work most effective.

I love the conversations that can develop on Facebook based on people's postings! Subjects like this always get me thinking – and sometimes even provide fodder for a column.

(For a more humorous 'take' on semicolons, check out a poem written and performed by a late friend of mine: go to http://www.youtube.com/user/ShoesTooDeep2 and look on the right for 'Colonoscopy.' The pertinent line is the last one. Enjoy!)

Take Those Zombies Out of Your Writing[4]

No, don't worry – not the characters from your stories. Rather, take whatever resembles the undead from your sentences so your writing will find new life. Good writing is good writing, whatever the genre and whomever the characters.

Continuing the zombie metaphor, let's explore one area to perk up one's writing. The first draft of what is now the first sentence in this paragraph read: "So how does one remove the zombie-like drooping skin and limping gait from one's writing, metaphorically speaking?"

A better version, in my opinion, is to re-work the sentence to read, "How does one remove from one's writing any skin that droops and gait that limps …?"

---

[4]This has the title it does because it was written for an online writing group that LOVED zombies. Vampires and other horror characters were also active among the various stories, poems, contests, small groups, conversations about favorite books and movies, etc., but zombies were, by far, the favorites. I also had zombies on my mind because I had set myself the task of writing about them, to stretch my capabilities to see if I could complete an original short story about zombies without giving up. I did just that, and – if I do say so myself – it wasn't half bad.

The difference is in the gerunds. According to www.wisegeek.com, "a gerund ... stems from a verbal, or a verb form, but does not act as a verb in a sentence ... A gerund is a verbal that functions as a noun ... [and] without exception ... always ends in *–ing.*"

WiseGeek uses this example: "My dog's favorite pastime is *sleeping.*" That's a good example of a gerund, but to me that's lazy writing, writing that hobbles around like the undead. My suggestion to spark new life into the sentence? Take the gerund out entirely, make it more active, and write, "My dog loves to sleep. It's his/her favorite pastime."

Somewhere long ago in the haze of grammar classes in junior high school, I remember a teacher's dictum that gerunds tend to be passive. That in turn slows down speech and writing. If you want your zombies – or the people who run from them – to get the readers' attention, then take out as many instances of *–ing* as possible.

Here's another example, this one from a newspaper feature story: *"'We'll be using people in a lot of different ways,' she says."* Of course the writer of the article had to quote the person with her own words, but if she could have re-worked it, this is better: "We intend to use people in a lot of different ways." Now the impact is at once more active, definitive and immediate, and it holds more promise.

Some gerunds are necessary – as you'll see in those I've left in here – but many are not. It takes a little more effort and sometimes a few more words to take out the lazy undead buggers from our writing, but it's always worth it. The zombies who remain in your stories will thank you for rejuvenating their drooping – oops! — *droopy* skin, and so will your readers.

The point is to go over your work to search for writing that just plods along. Our *intent* is rarely lazy, but sometimes we write that way, especially because we are so used to what I call "social network language" – which is rife with passive–*ing* status reports – and sound bites. We want our work to be different from that.

Sometimes the difference is subtle. If a gerund makes a good impact, then keep it in. If not, toss it, like any right-minded zombie hunter. If you don't, editors from prospective publications surely will, or should.

Good grammar appropriately used always gives new life to the undead in our sentences and paragraphs. There's nothing like writing that sparkles and has a good pace. Then our prose, poems and stories will shine as well. Even zombies want their writing to be noticed for the right reason.

Letter to Ford Motor Company

For years I've suffered through Ford's print and television advertisements. Today I finally did something about it.

If you've read my page about apostrophes, 'Apostrophe Alert,' you know the story of a late friend who was an apostrophe vigilante. Well, I've taken a page from her book and written to the advertising department at Ford Motor Company about their ads that proclaim 'Go further.'

While there are no apostrophes in that tagline, there *is* a grammatical error. Simply put, it should read 'Go farther,' and that's what I wrote today in an email to Ford.

If you think about it, it's a matter of distance. I presume Ford wants their customers to drive far in their vehicles. So one should say 'farther.' One does not say, for instance, 'You'll go fur,' but 'You'll go far.' 'Further' is a philosophical construct — 'I'll have to think about that further,' for instance, for 'I'll have to think about that some more.'

Of course, I have no idea if my one email will make a difference in Ford's ads, but stranger things are known to happen. Since we're talking about English here, it's possible — even likely — there are exceptions to my assertion, but I'm pretty sure it's safe to say that if we remember the 'fur/far' distinction, our writing will be correct — in this instance, anyway — and customers will send *us* letters of praise.

After I sent my email to Ford's Communications Department, I heard back from a nice young woman almost immediately. Wow, I was impressed ... until I read the conclusion of her response, the upshot of which was that 'Go further' was Ford's corporate brand, had been for years, and that's what people expected so it would not be changed. I responded to her response with thanks, of course, and reiterated my grammatical stand. Soon after that, she wrote again to say that any brand ideas and/or changes come from in-house corporate people only. So I thanked her again and let it go. Obviously there won't be any grammar changes from Ford, but at least I tried.

Different Strokes: How Do You Work Best?

Note: A short time after I posted this online, I realized I'd already published it with a different title. I was going to take it down, but I received a comment or two immediately and decided to keep it up. In the interim, I had the opportunity to read an article about something very similar, which bears out — and says better and in more detail — what I was trying to express. The article can be found at NPR.com. Look for the title 'In a Digital Chapter, Paper Notebooks are as Relevant as Ever' from May 27, 2015. Be sure to read the comments, too!

Do you have or utilize different writing/creative processes for the different genres in which you write?

When I write poetry, for instance, I have to start and finish the first draft in longhand. Once I start refining a poem, I can do it on the computer – though it always seems better when I stick to pen and paper – but it always has to start with the physical process. The pen has to channel my images and thoughts onto paper. And I need silence. Lots and lots of silence, and no distractions.

When I write fiction, I usually start that same way, but then I can easily go to the computer or go back and forth between the two as I craft the final product. Again I need silence for this, but there can be the (rare) occasional and short-lived distraction.

Creative non-fiction is the easiest to compose on the computer, for some reason. And I can work on something with other things going on around me.

I've always been intrigued at these differences. So here's the question: *How do you work best in your various genres and why?*

What is a Poem?

What is poetry? What makes a poem a poem and not prose or a song?

Here's a common complaint about poetry: It's the oldest form of expression, but what can it do for us now, in an age of social media, Twitter, Facebook and national urgency?

Claudia Rankin, Chancellor of the Academy of American Poets

This discussion began a few years ago between a person who does not like or understand poetry and me. The questions above are his. As a lifelong (almost) poet, I could go on for hours as I try to explain what poetry is. What follows, then, are some collected thoughts in response, to get the conversation started.

Samuel Taylor Coleridge declared poetry to be "the best words in the best order."

Rainer Maria Rilke wrote of image and allusion, and concentrated, condensed emotion and experience.[5]

---

[5] I'm not sure where this comes from. It's either in *Letters to a Young Poet,* or in the collection of Rilke's work that is translated by Stephen Mitchell.

A friend of mine who is a powerful and profound poet asserts that a poem is the right words for the right occurrence.

Rackham and Bertagnolli respond to Wordsworth's claim that "poetry is a 'spontaneous overflow of emotion,'" by saying that "no writing, not even poetry, is ever totally spontaneous."[6] Yet Robert Frost is known for saying a poem "begins with a lump in the throat."

Someone else has written that

> ... Poetry is a break for freedom. In a sense all poems are good; all poems are an emblem of courage and the attempt to say the unsayable; but only a few are able to speak to something universal yet personal and distinct at the same time; to create a door through which others can walk into what previously seemed unobtainable realms, in the passage of a few short lines.[7]

Mary Oliver writes that "Poetry isn't a profession, it's a way of life. It's an empty basket; you put your life into it and make something."

Another Robert Frost thought: "Poetry is about the grief. Politics is about the grievance." Perhaps that's the difference between poetry and prose too? As much as prose can be written poetically, it's still a different 'creature' with a different intent. As W. B. Yeats explains, "Out of the quarrel with others, we make rhetoric; out of the quarrel with ourselves we make poetry."

---

[6]*From Sight to Insight, 5.*
[7] Unattributed introduction to the Website of David Whyte, at www.davidwhyte.bigmindcatalyst.com

I suggest, too, that the difference between the two is the 'white space.' Poetry is more about what's left out, what I call poetic silence, to be intuited, already known – like haiku writers leave room for the reader to finish the creation – whereas prose tends to spell it out for us. If "Fiction is the truth inside the lie," as Stephen King asserts, is there a poetic correlation? According to Allen Ginsburg, "Poetry is the one place where people can speak their original human mind. It is the outlet for people to say in public what is known in private."

Robert Penn Warren believes "The poem is a little myth of man's capacity of making life meaningful. And in the end, the poem is not a thing we see – it is, rather, a light by which we may see – and what we see is life." As Sylvia Plath says, "I write only because there is a voice within me that will not be still."

I wrote my first poem at age six (I still have that little poem somewhere), so I've called myself a poet for over 50 years. I believe there is what I call a 'poetic sensibility,' a way of looking at life, of understanding life, of getting through the hard times, of celebrating the joys in ways no other form of writing can do, in my humble opinion.

In fact, I agree with Sharon Olds, who writes of poetry, "I would hate to imagine living without it. It's where I discover what I think and feel and make something of it."

It is spring again. The earth is like a child that knows
poems by heart. – Rainer Marie Rilke

Two Must-Have Books

I want to suggest a couple of books that are or should be like bibles for writers of any genre.[8] Though the subject matter for these books is primarily non-fiction, there is considerable fodder for the other genres as well. Because they're both so foundational, you might find they will also serve as a solid base for poetry.

The first book is William Zinsser's classic *On Writing Well: An Informal Guide to Writing Nonfiction.* I have the third edition (NY: Harper & Row, 1988), but I'm sure there are newer editions out by now.

Zinsser's style is indeed informal and easy to read. At the same time it's provocative. He starts off with a comparison between his answers to a group of students and teachers, about writing and the writer's life and vocation, and those of a newly-emerged writer-slash-surgeon. Though diametrically opposed to the other, each of their answers broadened the other's perspective.

" ... [A]t the heart of good nonfiction writing," Zinsser says as a result, "... come two of the most important qualities this book will go in search of: humanity and warmth. Good writing has an aliveness that keeps the

---

[8] There are, of course, many other books from which to choose and to utilize (to say nothing of online resources). One beside me now is *Woe is I: The Grammarphobe's Guide to Better English in Plain English* by Patricia T. O'Connor (NY: Riverhead Books, 1996/2003). Like Kilpatrick, O'Connor makes grammar issues fun, even understandable. She's a good writer, though the internal design and typefaces are, to me, distracting.

reader reading from one paragraph to the next, and it's not a question of gimmicks to 'personalize' the author. It's a question of using the English language in a way that will achieve the greatest strength and the least clutter.

"Can such principles be taught?" he asks. "Maybe not. But most of them can be learned" (pgs. 5, 6).

Zinsser proceeds, then, to address such things as simplicity, clutter, style, the audience, words, and usage. That first part – entitled 'Principles' – is followed by 'Forms' and 'Approaches,' which explore 'Nonfiction as the New American Literature,' the techniques of the lead-in and the end, interviews, science, technical and business writing, humor, sports, criticism, and writing about place. His chapter on using a word processor is likely outdated now (though, no doubt, this is taken care of in newer editions), but his concluding chapters on 'Trust Your Material' and 'Write as Well as You Can' are important.

The chapter on "Bits and Pieces," what Zinsser calls "scraps and morsels [and] small admonitions" (pg. 110), is strong and necessary for every writer. Some quick highlights: "Verbs are the most important of all your tools." "Most adverbs are unnecessary." "Most adjectives are also unnecessary." "Prune out the small words that qualify how you feel ... think and what you saw ..." "Don't overstate." "Your subconscious mind does more writing than you think." "Don't ever hesitate to imitate another writer ... But pick only the best models" (pgs. 100-132).

James J. Kilpatrick's *Fine Print: Reflections on the Writing Art* is just as easy to read as Zinsser's book, but it's a lot funnier. While Zinsser was a professor at Yale, Kilpatrick was a syndicated columnist and television commentator with a rapid-fire wit and – like Zinsser – a deep love of language. Kilpatrick's first chapter, in fact, starts right there: it's called "How Must We Write? *Con Amore!*"

Much of *Fine Print* is taken from people's responses to his decades' worth of newspaper reporting and columns around politics, nature, and writing. He also responds to some of his own and others' writing foibles and accomplishments. There is much to learn in this first half of the book – and he, too, delves into some of the techniques that will help any writer.

The best part, though (at least in this writer-editor's humble opinion), comes in the second part. Called "My Crotchets and Your Crotchets," Kilpatrick deals with his own and others' pet peeves (mostly his own) in what he calls "an unauthorized forum" from which he learned "from the peeves and the irks ..." and "trot[s] out [his] own little crotchets for inspection" (pg . 130). Going from A to Z, he looks at spelling, correct and incorrect usages, slang, the differences in popular words and how they are correctly used (such as 'affect' and 'effect,' 'blatant' and 'flagrant,' 'farther' and 'further,' 'less' and 'fewer') all the way through the alphabet.

Kilpatrick's sense of humor shines through here, even more so than in the first section. He admits to being something of a snob when it comes to language, but he earned that self-appellation because he was a phenomenal, sensitive and effective writer. His humor just makes his admonitions and declarations easy to take and learn from. His declaration on the usage of 'irregardless' is short and pithy: "Take my word for it: There is no such word. Yes, it is in the dictionaries, but *there is no such word*" (pg. 202). Even the computer's spell check feature agrees with him.

Here's his take on a common mistake with the words 'nauseated' and 'nauseous' (pg. 221):

"It is more trouble than it's worth to define and to defend this little troublemaker. Careful writers, writing careful paragraphs, will want to reserve *nauseous* in the sense of obnoxious, repulsive, or repellent. To say that someone is *nauseous* is to say something extremely unkind.

"To say that someone is *nauseated* is to say that the poor person is about to emulate George Bush in Japan. A lady or a gentleman who is nauseated will soon recover, but one who is nauseous may stay that way forever."

Both books will 'work' for any genre, but *Fine Print* is much broader in scope and will probably help more because Kilpatrick was more of a craftsman and artist than Zinsser. There's nothing wrong with laughing as one writes, after all!

There is much to learn in each of these gems, so I urge you to run right out to your nearest bookstore or Amazon.com and get yourself a copy of each (even before – *gasp!* — *Strunk's and White's* or other stylebooks). Not only are they both good resources to consult when needed, they're just plain fun to read.

If you can get only one now, I suggest Kilpatrick's book. You'll probably have to special order it because it's out of print, but do so. I can guarantee it's worth the effort. They both are, and these bibles will grace both your desk and your writing.

© ERR January 2010 (This first appeared in the KeyPub.net ezine)

Critiques and Reviews Workshop

Critique/Reviews Workshop Outline and Notes

(Based on and expanded from ideas for a workshop in an online writing group from several years ago, with thanks and a hat tip to my friend, author Rob Read)

The intent of reviews/critiques is to benefit the writing, characters, plot – and thereby all of us as writers – not to criticize authors or their writing. The story/poem/essay/etc., is the focus, NOT the person who has done the writing. There's a reason 'critique' is not spelled 'criticism.'

Following are some thoughts on what makes for a good review experience, from and for both writers and reviewers. Of course correct spelling, grammar/syntax, and punctuation are givens!

Notes for authors who request reviews of their work:

1) Post work in manageable sections. If the work is longer than, say, 1000 words, split into multiple posts. Some sites allow for 'Read more' breaks, too, which can be inserted at any point.

2) Add links, if possible, at bottom for next / previous entries on multiple posts.

3) Thank reviewers who take the time to read and review your work.

4) Plan ahead to try not to take offence. The review is only the opinion of the reviewer, but even supposedly negative feedback – warranted or not – can be helpful.

5) State any areas you want reviewers to pay attention to, or to ignore.

6) State the intended audience and the genre, especially if those could be unclear.

7) A personal peeve here: I suggest writers NOT post their pieces in color or in fancy or tiny font. This is particularly true for longer pieces. My own aging eyes find it hard to read such posts when, for instance, red, blue, or purple typeface is placed against a black background, especially if the font is smaller than 12-point size, and I know I'm not the only one for whom this is true. Keep to the tried and true black-on-white.

Notes for reviewers:

1) Make sure the author of the work is aware that the review is your opinion only.

2) Critique must be constructive, not criticism or critical. In other words ...

3) *Review the writing, not the author.*

4) Be diplomatic and respectful. Replace statements like 'You must ...', 'You cannot ...', 'You should ...' with 'I feel it might be better to say ...', or 'Do you think it might be worded better if ...', or 'What if you tried ...'. 'I statements' and the equivalent are always better – 'The descriptive paragraph at the top of page 28 makes me feel ... because ...'

5) Give the good points of the review. Critiques are intended to be positive and to address the positive fully as much as the areas that need work. This is what I call a critique sandwich: insert the suggestions of what can be improved between two layers of what already works.

6) Review as you would like to be reviewed. Give reasons for your suggestions and comments. 'I love this poem!' isn't a review, nor is 'Such and such might work better' without saying why.

7) Read carefully, making notes of your first impression. For an in-depth review, read more than once before responding.

8) Write your review before reading other reviews.

9) Consider who the author is writing for, the readership of the finished work. How does s/he succeed (or not)?

Guidelines for what to review and what authors should pay attention to as they write

Most of these are for fiction but can be applied to other genres as well:

1) Does the opening hook work, and did the writing hold your attention?

2) Are the characters alive, believable? This is just as important in creative non-fiction, especially memoir.

3) If fiction, do the storyline, plot and sub-plots flow in logical sequence? Are they believable?

4) If fiction, is the description of locale detailed enough, depending whether the work is a short story or chapter from a novel? How to discern 'detailed enough' and too much detail? Think about the pacing: does the story move along? Are there parts that get sluggish? If so, why? How does the character development help or hinder?

5) Does the dialogue between and among characters sound natural yet give the reader necessary information? Is there enough dialogue? Too much? Keep in mind that dialogue is one technique to 'show, not tell.' When done well, it's quite effective and helps with pacing.

6) Is the point of view (POV) clear as to who is speaking? If not, what can help?

7) Do the tenses correspond throughout? Active voice is one of the best ways to keep up a good pace in any writing, fiction and nonfiction. This doesn't mean you can't use past tense – past tense and passive voice are not the same thing. Almost all 'ing'[9] words are passive and slow the reader. Sometimes it's called for, but it should be used sparingly.

8) If the piece is fiction and calls for readers' 'willing suspension of belief' for an effective plot, does the author succeed? How so?

9) In fiction, do the characters 'earn' their places and points in the story for a right/effective conclusion? In other words, does the author speed things up to get over a difficult time period or plot inconvenience, or does s/he take the time to let the characters live their own stories without such contrivances as 'A few months later …' that move things

---

[9] See my discussion about gerunds in the chapter above entitled 'Take Those Zombies Out of Your Writing'

along too fast by telling rather than showing? Let readers 'live' with the characters. What have we missed in those 'few months'? If there are hurdles or timeframes that need to be navigated, show us how the characters do it, and what they think and how they feel as they do so.

Those Fulsome Wordplay Blues

Yes, English can be weird. It can be understood through tough thorough thought, though.[10]

It's been said that English is one of the most difficult languages to learn to speak and even harder to learn to write and spell. With such words to choose among as famous/infamous, bear/bare, and their/they're/there, I can understand why. As a freelance editor and writing mentor, I see some doozies, but at least I can edit those. What really drives me crazy are those I read in already-published books, stories and newspapers. Seems those respective editors need editors themselves ...

Let's get a jump, then, on the seemingly-clueless editors and, at the same time, impress prospective readers, agents, and the editors who *do* have a clue and who will read your submitted works. What follows is a small sampling of the myriad word mangles I've come across recently, in print and in conversation.

Famous/Infamous: If a person, place or thing is well-known s/he/it is famous. If said person, place or thing is known for something(s) that goes against (shall we say) the common good, then s/he/it is infamous. Example: *Golf phenom Tiger Woods is arguably among the most famous*

---

[10] Unattributed meme on Facebook.

people in the world. I think it's fair to say, given his fall from grace last year, that his ... um ... antics can be described as infamous. (Which then begs the question: is he now infamously famous or famously infamous? I'm not sure I can wrap my brain around that one!)

Plutonic/Platonic: This one came up in conversation a while ago when someone told me a relationship he was in was Plutonic. Though I realize some relationships can seem like they're in orbit or cause one to feel at one among the stars, relationships are Platonic only.

It's/Its: The apostrophe belongs *only* in the contraction for 'it is.' *Learning which is which will be worth its weight in gold, though it's (it is) often hard to tell the difference.*

Your/You're: Similarly the apostrophe belongs *only* for the contraction of 'you are.' *You're (you are) bound to come across these in your work all the time, so it's important to get them right!*

Their/There/They're: This set of words causes problems for folks who are familiar with the English language and its whims of spelling and syntax, fully as much as for those who are unfamiliar with all the intricacies. Unfortunately there's no little trick to help remember the differences, except with the apostrophe and the contraction. *Those folks are going to have trouble with their writing or when they're (they are) talking with folks over there unless they memorize this one.*

Between/Among: The general rule is that 'between' is for two people, places or things; 'among' is for three or more. *Between you and me*, I love to walk among the trees in the woods.*

Bare/Bear: My orbitally-challenged friend gets this one wrong all the time, too. *One bears a lot of responsibility when one bares one's soul. The ground is bare even as it bears the weight of the winter cold.*

Fulsome: If you receive fulsome praise, you are right to feel blue – or at least to wonder about the source. Though the word is often used to mean a good thing, it's not. According to the *Oxford Dictionary and Thesaurus,* 'fulsome' is defined as "disgusting by excess of flattery, servility, or expressions of flattery; cloying ... In *fulsome praise,* fulsome means 'excessive,' not 'generous.'" In his book *Fine Print: Reflections on the Writing Art* (which I review in the chapter 'Two Must-Have Books'), James J. Kilpatrick takes on the venerable *Oxford,* though – at least a little bit. Noting that it is not the "friendly" word he once thought it was, Kilpatrick maintains that "*Fulsome* does not mean abundant, or copious, or florid, *or excessive.* Its primary meaning is insincere, phony, *offensively* effusive ..." (my emphases).

Finally, while we still have ol' Jack here, this is what he thinks of the word '**irregardless**:' "Take my word for it: There is no such word. Yes, it is in the dictionaries, but *there is no such word.*" I will humbly submit, in agreement, that this no-such-word is the equivalent of a double negative and is, therefore, superfluous. Regardless of what the dictionaries say. Why add an extra syllable when it's not needed and it negates itself?

As writers we've played and worked with words all our lives. We've arranged them, rearranged them, and sometimes rearranged them yet again ... and again.

Though we've learned some tricks along the way, there are some things we just have to memorize for correct usages. The more attention we pay to these seemingly small pieces in our wordplay, the fewer blue pencils are needed, and that's always a good thing.

When in doubt, consult your faithful grammar or style books. Remember, too, that the green and red lines in word processing programs aren't always correct. Neither, apparently, are dictionaries!

*Note: This is correct. It is *not* – I repeat, **NOT** – 'between you and I.' See that discussion in the chapter, 'Me, Myself, and I.'

Guided Meditation

This dreary, rainy day and the soft music on TV have put me in a meditative mood, so I thought I'd post this piece I wrote a few years ago for a workshop.

The workshop never happened — the weather was horrendous — and the time of year was autumn, not summer, but I think the meditation is still appropriate. A Native American flute CD was supposed to play in the background, so find something similar or just as soothing to listen to. It's best if someone else can read this quietly for you. If that can't happen, read it over a few times first and then just listen to the music as you settle in and close your eyes ...

Relax into the music, let it refresh your spirit as you take a few minutes to release any demands on you or concerns you have. Take some slow, deep breaths and feel the oxygen regenerating your body.

We're going on a short journey together, to find our muses and to find our own unique voice.

By now you may see an aura behind your closed eyelids ... maybe a brilliant sunflower, stars, or flashes of green and blue lights. Enjoy them for a moment, thank them for starting your journey for you with such beauty.

As these slowly fade away, you see you're on a wide path deep in the woods. It's a crisp, invigorating day in the early fall. Sunlight streams through the trees, a breeze sends a shower of multi-colored leaves around you as you walk, and you spot a partridge gliding past you on feather-covered feet that make no sound at all.

As you enjoy the sounds of the leaves joining those that make the tapestry in which you move, you inhale the rich, fertile fragrances of damp earth, the humus of the pine duff, the whiff of wood smoke that reached you just now.

You've come to a small glade of hemlock, oak and beech trees and you spy a granite and marble boulder among the intertwining roots. It's as if the trees and the boulder are anchors for each other, holding the other into and onto the ground just for you. Near the granite ridge of the stone's top, there's an indentation that makes a comfortable place to sit.

So you sit ... and listen to the silence of no traffic, the rustling whisper the leaves make as they fall ... to the occasional bird murmurs, chattering of the red squirrel, squeaks of the chipmunks ... As the silence fills up around you, you hear the sound of water and discover this peaceful spot is just above a mountain stream, heavy from a recent rain, rushing over boulders and stones placed there eons ago by a glacier as it scoured the mountainside.

You take a deep, deep breath, enjoying the cool air that rises from the water below to meet the warm drafts of sunlighted breezes playing among the trees. You've slipped off the boulder seat onto the musty ground; lean now into the stone behind you and close your eyes ……

Sometime later you awaken. The sun is lower, the woodland creatures are quiet, even the breeze has stilled. You've lost all track of time, but you know it's that magical time when afternoon seems to hold its breath before it slides into dusk. It's time to start back.

You start to rise from your nest of ground and boulder ... and in doing so, your hand overturns a palm-sized stone smoothed and ridged from the stream. Then your foot dislodges another one of similar size. Turn them over to admire their simple yet complicated beauty, the marble veins gleaming in the late sunshine tilting through the trees, and appreciate their soft heft and weight.

When you turn them over, you find there is writing, something roughly etched as if with a smaller, sharper stone or knife, or maybe woodland faery spirits. A close look reveals a word on each: "Voice" on one, "Sing" on the other.

Curious now, you kneel to dig a little more and find an irregular circle of similar stones underneath the leaves, each with its own word. You place the first two stones inside the indentation on the boulder, and each subsequent stone finds its place there as well. The stone words include 'Risk,' 'Promise,' 'Empty,' 'Find' ... and there are several more.

Without intending to, you realize you've made a poem as you placed the stones onto the boulder. Perhaps this is where they started, then, after that unknown person or spirit scraped these words and placed them on the altar of the boulder near the stream. Perhaps a squirrel or a heavy wind sent them into hiding, to wait for you to find them.

You place the last stone in the center of the circle, its word "Gladness" uppermost, and you back away. It's time now to retrace your steps along the woodland path. You give thanks to the spirits of the woods, the stream, the stones and boulders, the creatures. Dusk is nearly here and you must be able to see your way out; but it seems that a light from behind you shines in just the places you need to put your feet.

It's the words, you think. They've made the way easier and brighter. When you come through the woods again, you turn around and the light is gone. Gone along the pathway, yes, but there is new light in your heart.

You stand there for a moment or two because you want to remember the poem you left back in the glade. You want to write that poem ... or song ... or paint a picture ... or tell a story ....

And you want to come back and add your own words for another person to find at the right time.

Place Names

Mesdames y Messieurs,

It's almost summer, and that means a lot of people will travel to various destinations across the country, around the world, or even just around town. What follows is based on a group exercise I suggested for an online writing group: a creative possibility using some of the famous place names of New Orleans.

I was born there, but my parents and I left when I was 18 months old and I've been back only once. Even if one has never been to the Crescent City, though, most everyone knows some of the names of the streets and places through song and literature.

There is, of course, Tennessee Williams' play – subsequently made into a movie – called *Streetcar Named Desire*.

And there's a book called *Frenchmen, Desire, Good, Children*, by John Chase, which was published in 1949. The title refers to four different streets in NOLA (but read it without the commas and you get another idea!). Of course there's also Bourbon, Canal, St. Charles, Rampart, Royal, Chartres, Orleans, Basin, Dauphine, Iberville ... and so many more. {Note: A politically correct person who reads the book will have trouble with the antiquated mentions of some groups of people, but for a history of New Orleans it's a good read that explains the colorful origins – and pronunciations – of the original street names.}

For all you travelers, then, here's an "assignment": Pay attention to the names that jump out at you and why.

When you get back, write a piece – even a travelogue – that incorporates the names that meant the most to you and explain why. Did they get you thinking, stir up old feelings or new possibilities? Are they related to someone you know or knew? In short, explore the creative possibilities from all the creative names in the Big Easy or any city, town, or village.

For those of us who remain homebound, we can do the same with the places around us. In our closer-to-home travelogues, which names are we drawn to and why? What do they evoke? What do we want others to know about these places that are so familiar to us?

Another option is to ponder why NOLA has so many 'nicknames' and write about that. I know of few other cities with so many and different monikers, and each has its own defining image. Does the same hold true for the places around you?

Or do you give names to certain places closer to home? When my sister and I were young, for instance, we had a couple of favorite 'roller coaster roads' on which we'd implore our dad to drive. (We never told him about the 'drag race road' we used later as teenagers …)

Sometimes it's as simple as being in the right place at the right time. After all, Tennessee Williams was inspired by the streetcar that ran right outside his door, and the rest is literary history.

Don't forget to try out your non-dominant hand for this, too. That'll really get the creative juices flowing like that beautiful, mighty and mysterious Mississippi River!

Wherever you go, then, safe travels on/in your planes, buses, trains, cars, *and* imaginations.

Everybody walks past a thousand story ideas a day. The good writers are the ones who see five or six of them. Most people don't see any.

Orson Scott Card

That Horn You Hear is Mine

Note: This is more a reminder to myself than blatant self-promotion. It's something of a written 'selfie,' I suppose, so read with that in mind, please. At the same time, I suggest each of us can benefit from doing a similar exercise once in a while. What, then, can you proclaim? What can you blow your own horn about? Let us hear it!

I usually shy away from using the pronoun 'I' to start anything I write, but today I'm going to use it on purpose because I'm going to blow my own horn.

I do that even less than I start my work with … you know … but here's why I'm doing both in this post: ***I'm a damn good editor***. There, both 'I's and the horn in one sentence. In bold italics, too. Wow!

I started thinking of this last week. I was in the hospital sleeping off (kind of) the general anesthesia I'd had earlier on Tuesday for a catheter ablation and, for some reason, I started thinking of all the people for whom I've served as editor. Then I started to recall all the different projects they have shared with me. This train of thought was inspired, I believe, by the teamwork of all the medical staff who worked on and with me for the procedure: the surgeon, of course, but also — and especially — the pre-op, OR, and post-op nurses and nursing assistants, the lab folks, the food service and housekeeping staffs, even the pre-op registrar.

We all need a team around us as we work — family, friends, colleagues to support and encourage us in our solitary writing times. As an editor, too, I prefer to work as a team with each particular author. I don't, and won't, work alone with another's words. I cannot presume to give voice to another's words and vision on my own, and so I relish the opportunity to get to know each author, to communicate with her on a regular basis, to make suggestions for him to consider, to offer ideas for us both to try together.

As I thought of all the years I've done this editing gig — this work that I love, and all the people, all the projects and manuscripts I've worked with — I realized that I am a team myself, too. The majority of good editors are, and we have to be, but it's according to a different definition of 'team.'

This team knows how to edit Steampunk stories, vampire novels, poetry collections, humorous and spiritual memoirs, academic papers and dissertations, essays and other creative non-fiction, fantasy and mainstream short stories, even pastoral theology for the various intended audiences because I have written in all of these — and other — genres. I know how to spell and punctuate according to British, Australian, Canadian *and* American customs from a lifetime of reading and studying a wide variety of world literature from the earliest of days to last week, along with the most up-to-date journals and manuals. In other words, then, I am backed up by the sometimes-centuries of unseen writers who have gone before me, on whose shoulders I am privileged to stand, and what they've taught me.

I am beyond grateful. I am also well aware that my own writing may not — and in some cases, does not — compare with some of the writers I've read over the years. The important thing in my teambuilding, though, is that I've tried my hand at the different genres. I made it a point to stretch myself, sometimes going beyond my comfort zone (as when I wrote zombie and vampire stories), for my own benefit, but especially to improve my editing work.

That's what teams do best: we encourage each other to reach beyond what is normal, what is usual. I've found that because I've done so myself, I can do so for others as well. Together, then, our work ensures my clients that their words are in good hands. They can entrust their words to me because ***I am a damn good editor.***

Afterword: A Writer's World

A writer is a world trapped inside a person.

Victor Hugo

I first coined 'hospitable writing' when I wrote an annotation on a book on sacred geometry I was supposed to read as part of my BA studies. I could not finish the book. While I expected mathematical terminology, given the context, there were too many instances where terms were not translated or explained for a non-mathematical audience. The typeface and font were far too small for aging eyes. The formatting was much too cramped, so there was virtually no white space, and the pages were printed on glossy paper, which meant the contrast was too stark. Overall it was not a good experience.

The etymology of 'hospitality' is related to the Old French and Old English words that go back to the Latin roots for 'hospice,' 'host,' and – not surprisingly – 'hospital.'[11] All of these words indicate the care of or for someone(s).

Ursula Le Guin has written that "A writer is a person who cares what words mean, what they say, how they say it. Writers know words are their way towards truth and freedom, and so they use them with care, with thought,

---

[11] *The Oxford Dictionary of Word Histories: The Life Stories of Over 12,000 Words.* GlynnisChantrell, ed. NY: Oxford University Press, 2002.

with fear, with delight." Isn't this another way of proclaiming hospitality? We are hosts who care for and about our guests, our readers. We welcome them into the 'homes' of our books, articles, poems, to be invigorated and inspired.

Remembering William Zinsser's proclamation, we work hard so they may rest easy in our words.

This book is just a start, something of a primer, a companion for you from the Website. There will likely be another volume at some point – I think two or more 'installments' are better, more hospitable, than a thick, heavy grammar book – and I will, of course, continue to add additional pages and posts to the Website: www.magiclampedots.wordpress.com. Thank you for coming to visit, and I hope you'll come back soon.

Thank you, especially, for being a writer who cares, for working hard to unlock the world inside you.

Appendix

ABOUT Magic Lamp
Editing Services

Magic Lamp Editing Services

by Genie

Hard writing makes easy reading. Easy writing makes hard reading.

(William Zinsser)

Entrust your words to someone who cares about them as much as you do. You've done the hard part – now I can work with you to make your writing a pleasure to read. I will help you:

- Erase sentence fragments (except where intended)
- Cite sources correctly in academic papers
- Develop characters' dialogue to 'show, don't tell'
- Rearrange text, sentences and chapters for better pacing and comprehension
- Format to submit for publication
- Accomplish your intent with appropriate spelling, punctuation and grammar
- Manuscript critiques (see below) – and much more

Jobs small and large

- Query letters and proposals
- Brochures and flyers
- Novels, short stories and other fiction
- Creative non-fiction
- Poetry
- Essays, academic papers and dissertations, annotations and annotated bibliographies
- Sermons
- Newsletters
- Line-by-line edits or suggested summary
- Website and blog narrative content (Please note: though I have no experience with HTML code or technical language, I can work with you on the narrative text you plan to include on your site. In some cases I can also help with formatting.)
- Almost anything you can think of to write. Please inquire!

Individual contractual agreements, crafted with and for you, are based on your project needs. I provide professional, thoughtful, quick yet comprehensive edits (and critique, if desired) *that maintain your unique voice*. I work with both online (Word and Open Office) and hard copy manuscripts, by email or postal mail, whichever you prefer.

Fees are per project or by the hour, based on my initial review, and payment schedules can be negotiated.

Manuscript Critiques

Detailed and comprehensive summary of suggested edits, including comments and ideas: $1.75/page.

Initial and general impressions: $1.00/page.

About Me

A writer for over 50 years, I am the author of fiction, non-fiction, creative non-fiction, and poetry. With a BA in holistic studies, an MA in writing and creative studies, and a post-graduate diploma in theology, I have a wide range of experience and interests. I have been privileged to serve as an academic and writing mentor for undergrad and graduate students. In addition to co-founding a regional collective of spoken word and musical artists, I served as senior editor at and wrote a regular column on self-editing tips for an online writing ezine.

I am also the co-founder of Branch Hill Publications, a small indie print-on-demand company that has published almost two dozen books since we started in 2011. My short fiction, non-fiction and poetry are in print and online media, and my novel and the CNF book I co-authored are available on Amazon.com and for Kindle. I am currently working on a new novel (the first in an occasional series), as well as three poetry chapbooks.

Contact:

Genie Rayner, Bennington VT

802-681-7071 or magiclampedits@gmail.com

And look for and share Magic Lamp Editing Services on Facebook!

Making Connections: Linking Up

This page is for links to other authors' pages and Websites, notable news reports that are pertinent to writing, grammar, editing, and related subjects, occasional (but limited) self-promotional announcements, creativity, the literary world, and more. At the time this book goes to print, this list is up to date. Please check the Magic Lamp Website for new additions as they happen.

Publishing/Publishers

Branch Hill Publications:

http://branchhillpublications.weebly.com. We publish almost all genres (check Website to be sure before submitting), and our new imprint, Tehom Books, focuses on issues of social justice. A catalogue of all the books we've published, and those that are coming soon, is on the Website, as are guidelines for submission and more.

Blooming Twig Books: http://bloomingtwig.com/ — From the Website: 'Award-winning indie press. We publish books that matter.' Founder and CEO: Kent Gustavson.

Authors, Writers, Poets

Lori R. Lopez: http://www.fairyflyentertainment.com. Lori is a remarkable storyteller, poet and artist. Her stellar imagination takes flight with words that are fresh and invigorating and will take your breath away.

C. Susan Nunn: http://www.csusannunn.com. Author of *Song of the Earth*, Susan's site and blog feature opportunities to participate in her in-person and online workshops on 'place in writing' and feng shui for writers.

Sirrah Medeiros, at http://www.sirrahmedeiros.com, is a writer and poet with strong ties to the military — both she and her husband are retired from the US Marines — and who often writes about science and the environment.

New York Times

Go to NYTimes.com to sign up for a free newsletter that lets you take a peek at the latest Review of Books (and archives). The Books Update newsletter comes to your email inbox every Friday, and the subscription entitles you to view ten (10) articles a month.

Blogs and Websites

withoutbullshit.com is a writing blog by Josh Bernoff. His May 4, 2015 edition, '10 top writing tips,' is definitely worth a visit. Be sure to read the comments, too, especially the give-and-take between Bernoff and some of his readers who take issue with a few of his assertions.

http://academia.stackexchange.com/questions/15595/why-are-so-many-badly-written-papers-still-published. Self-explanatory!

TheLiteracySite.com. A good source for inspiration and learning.

http://www.iauthor.com. Sources and resources for writers. Based in the UK but has links all over the world.

http://www.fundsforwriters.com . Free newsletter (with an option to pay for more detailed information) with editorials, firsthand experiences, tips, and info about conferences, contests, agents, markets.

poets.org: The Academy of American Poets.

TheSunMagazine.org. An outstanding – and ad-free – monthly collection of essays, memoirs, interviews, short stories, poetry, and photographs.

Blatant self-promotion

My first novel, *Song of the Blessing Trees,* is on Amazon and Kindle. It can also be ordered from the publisher at http://gileadbooks.com/catalogue.php?uid=157. From the blurb: 'Global warming is touching the lives of millions. This blend of fantasy, mythic experience, and science fiction is for people who care deeply about the well-being of the earth and anyone who wants a different view on a critical subject. As the Woods Clan's environment changes, they — and their ancestors Old Grandmother Gwynnyth and the Chronicler — are challenged to adapt to spiritual difficulties and physical hardships as they search out new and safer places to live.' Look for it under my full name, Eugenie R. Rayner.

My other blogs are http://ladybirch.wordpress.com and http://amusingplace.wordpress.com. It's been a long time since I've updated them, but I will soon, and they're still online if you're interested. The first is something like a journal, and the second is some of my poetry.

My second novel, *A Proud Little Town* (the first in an occasional series), is still in process, but I expect to finish the first draft by the fall of 2015.

Selected Bibliography

In addition to the books mentioned in the text, here are a few more resources that are and have been important for my work as both writer and editor.There are many others, but these are representative. The asterisks indicate books that are especially good, in my opinion.

Bernays, Anne and Pamela Painter. *What If? Exercises for Fiction Writers.* NY: HarperCollins Publishers, 1990.

Blanchard, Margaret and S. W. Sowbel. *Restoring the Orchard: A Guide to Learning Intuition.* Fort Ann, NY: Tara Press, 1994.

Blanchard, Margaret, ed. *From the Listening Place: Languages of Intuition.* Portland, ME: Astarte Shell Press, 1997.

Blanchard, Margaret. *The Rest of the Deer: An Intuitive Study of Intuition.* Portland, ME: Astarte Shell Press, 1993.*

Budbill, David. *Judevine*, rev. ed. White River Junction: Chelsea Green Publishing Co., 1999.

_____. *Moment to Moment: Poems of a Mountain Recluse.* Port Townsend, WA: Copper Canyon Press, 1998.*

Calderwood, James L. and Harold E. Toliver, eds. *Forms of Poetry.* Englewood Cliffs, NJ: Prentice-Hall, Inc., 1968.*

Dillard, Annie. *The Writing Life.* NY: HarperCollins Publications, 1989.

Fox, John. *Finding What You Didn't Lose: Expressing Your Truth and Creativity Through Poem-Making.* NY: Tarcher/Putnam, 1995.

_____. *Poetic Medicine: The Healing Art of Poem-Making.* NY: Tarcher/Putnam, 1997.

Ghiselin, Brewster, ed. *The Creative Process.* NY: New American Library, 1952.*

Kohl, Herbert. *A Grain of Poetry: How to Read Contemporary Poems and Make Them a Part of Your Life.* NY: HarperCollins Publishers, Inc., 1999.

Lamott, Anne. *Bird by Bird: Some Instructions on Writing and Life.* NY: Anchor Books, 1994.*

May, Rollo. *The Courage to Create.* W.W. Norton & Co., 1975.*

Mitchell, Stephen, ed. and trans. *The Selected Poetry of Rainer Maria Rilke.* NY: Vintage International, 1989.*

Moon, Janell. *Stirring the Waters: Writing to Find Your Spirit.* Boston: Journey Editions, 2001.

Nelson, G. Lynn. *Writing and Being: Taking Back Our Lives Through the Power of Language.* Philadelphia: Innisfree Press, 1994.

Oliver, Mary. *A Poetry Handbook: A Prose Guide to Understanding and Writing Poetry.* NY: Harcourt Brace and Co., 1994.*

_____. *New and Selected Poems.* Boston: Beacon Press, 1992.

_____. *Why I Wake Early.* Boston: Beacon Press, 2004.

_____. *Winter Hours: Prose, Prose Poems, and Poems.* Boston: Houghton Mifflin Co., 1999.

Rico, Gabriele Lusser. *Pain and Possibility: Writing Your Way Through Personal Crisis.* NY: Tarcher/Putnam, 1991.*

Rilke, Rainer Maria. *Letters to a Young Poet.* Trans. Stephen Mitchell. NY: Random House, 1984.

Schneider, Pat. *Writing Alone and With Others.* NY: Oxford University Press, 2003.*

_____. *How the Light Gets In: Writing As a Spiritual Practice.* NY: Oxford University Press, 2013.*

Smyth, Joshua M. and James W. Pennebaker. "Sharing One's Story: Translating Emotional Experiences into Words as a Coping Tool." *Coping: The Psychiatry of What Works*, C. R. Snyder, ed. NY: Oxford University Press, 1999. 70-89.

Szymborska, Wisława. *View With a Grain of Sand: Selected Poems.* StanisławBarańczak and Claire Cavanagh, trans. NY: Harcourt Brace and Co., 1995.*

Whyte, David. *The House of Belonging.* Langley, WA: Many Rivers Press, 2004.

Wooldridge, Susan Goldsmith. *Poemcrazy: Freeing Your Life With Words.* NY: Three Rivers Press, 1996.

Woolf, Virginia. *A Room of One's Own.* NY: Harcourt, Inc., 1929/1957. Foreward by Mary Gordon 1981.

A-ZBook   Reviewsbreaks columnscreative processCreativitycritique drafts editing Exercise genres grammar impatient/patient novelpetpeevespoemsprocrastinationtravelWelcome

writing